The Country Kit

Making Apple Pies & Crusts

by Phyllis Hobson

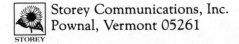

Storey Communications, Inc.
Pownal, Vermont 05261

CONTENTS

APPLE PIE

"As American as apple pie" is quite a compliment. For apple pie is practical, a nutritious, filling dish that makes good use of supplies on hand.

Apple pie is versatile: Vary the crust, the topping or the spices; slice the apples, chop them, sauce them; serve as pie a la mode. Variety is the spice of apple pie.

Apple pie is dependable. It doesn't rise or fall or stick to the pan. Any way you make it, you can't go wrong.

Apple pie is thrifty. In season, apples are inexpensive or even free for the picking. Add a little sweetening, a bit of crust and a dab of imagination and you have dessert at almost no cost. With all these qualities in its favor, what other dish would practical, versatile, dependable, thrifty Americans claim as their special own?

Many of the recipes that follow originated in pioneer days when every family homestead had at least one apple tree which was the source of between-meal treats, of spicy apple butter and shimmering clear jelly, of jugs of cider for drinking and bottles of vinegar for making pickles, of chewy dried apple slices and strips of sweet apple leather.

But most of all it was the source of the family's favorite dish — apple pie.

Most of the apple recipes in this book may be adapted to other fruits with a few simple adjustments. For the juicier

2

fruits, such as berries, double the thickening (flour, cornstarch, or tapioca.) For the more tart fruits, such as cherries, add half again as much sweetener (sugar or honey). Pears or peaches may be substituted for the apples called for in the recipe, with no other change in ingredients.

So go ahead and experiment. Mix, match and change as you please to use the fruits in season. But don't say we didn't warn you, for nothing is quite as good as apple pie.

THE PIES

Some of these apple pie recipes have been handed down from mother to daughter, from aunt to niece and have never been published before. Some appeared in very old cookbooks, written for another generation.

We present them to you here — modernized only where necessary, simplified and alphabetized — all in apple pie order.

AMISH APPLE PIE

3 cups diced apples
2/3 cup sugar
1 tablespoon flour
½ teaspoon cinnamon or nutmeg
2 tablespoons rich milk
2 tablespoons butter
Pastry for two 9-inch crusts
Mix apples, sugar, flour and spice until well blended.

Pour into unbaked crust. Sprinkle with milk and dot with bits of butter. Top with pie crust, seal edges and bake 50 minutes in 400-degree oven.

APPLE PIE

6 tart apples
1 cup sugar
¼ teaspoon salt
½ teaspoon cinnamon
2 tablespoons tapioca
2 tablespoons butter
2 teaspoons lemon juice

Line a pie pan with unbaked crust. Peel, core and thinly slice apples, placing half of them in the crust. Combine the sugar, salt, spice and tapioca and pour over the apples in the crust. Dot with butter, then add remaining apples and dribble with lemon juice. Cover with top crust and bake 10 minutes in a 450-degree oven, then 30 minutes at 375 degrees.

OR:

6 to 8 apples
1½ tablespoons flour
2/3 cup sugar
¼ teaspoon salt
¼ teaspoon powdered cinnamon
1½ tablespoons butter
grated peel of ½ lemon
Pastry for two 9-inch crusts

Peel, core and slice apples. Over the bottom of the crust sprinkle half the flour. Arrange half the apple slices over the flour, then sprinkle with half the sugar mixed with the cinnamon and salt. Add remaining apples and sprinkle with remaining flour, sugar and salt. Dot with butter. Mix grated lemon peel with the water and sprinkle over the apples. Cover with remaining pastry and seal edges well. Bake 15 minutes at 450 degrees then 30 minutes at 350 degrees. Serve warm with cheese or ice cream.

APPLE PIE WITH CRUMB TOPPING

3 cups apples, chopped fine
1 cup sugar
2 tablespoons flour
¼ teaspoon cinnamon
½ cup brown sugar
1/3 cup flour
3 tablespoons butter

Mix chopped apples with the 1 cup sugar, 2 tablespoons flour and cinnamon. Place in an unbaked pie crust and bake 10 minutes in 450-degree oven. Remove from oven and add topping made by mixing remaining three ingredients until crumbly. Return to oven and bake 30 minutes at 350-degrees.

APPLE PIE WITH ORANGE SAUCE

6 tart apples
½ cup sugar
¼ cup orange marmalade
2 tablespoons flour
2 tablespoons lemon juice
3 tablespoons butter

Slice apples into a mixing bowl. Add all remaining ingredients except butter. Mix well, then pour into unbaked pie crust and dot with butter. Cover with top crust and bake 10 minutes at 450 degrees, then 30 to 40 minutes at

350 degrees. Serve with Orange Sauce:
  1 cup water
  1 cup sugar
  3 tablespoons frozen orange juice concentrate
  Combine sugar and water. Cook 10 minutes over low heat, stirring often. Remove from heat and add orange concentrate. Stir to mix well. Spoon over each serving of pie.

APPLE PIE WITH PINEAPPLE SAUCE

Slice 6 tart apples into an unbaked pie crust. Without adding anything else, top with crust, leaving a round hole in the top. Bake 40 to 45 minutes in a 350-degree oven, or until apples are tender and crust is brown.

One-half hour before pie is done, combine in a saucepan:
  3 tablespoons grated fresh or frozen pineapple
  1 tablespoon water
  3 tablespoons sugar
  Simmer until the fruit is clear and the sauce is thickened. Take pie from oven and carefully pour sauce through hole in top. Set aside to cool.

APPLE BUTTER PIE

½ cup apple butter
2 eggs
½ cup sugar
1½ tablespoons cornstarch
1 teaspoon cinnamon
2 cups milk
Pastry for two 9-inch crusts
  Combine beaten eggs, sugar, cornstarch, cinnamon

and apple butter. Beat well. Gradually add milk and blend. Pour into crust. Cut remaining pastry into ¼-inch wide strips and place on top of pie lattice fashion. Bake 35 minutes at 375 degrees.

APPLE CAKE PIE

6 tart apples, sliced
1 teaspoon lemon juice
¾ cup sugar
¼ cup butter
1 egg, beaten
½ cup flour
½ teaspoon baking powder
¼ teaspoon salt

Arrange apple slices in unbaked pie crust and sprinkle with lemon juice and ¼ cup sugar. Cream butter and ½ cup sugar until fluffy. Add egg and beat well. Add flour, baking powder and salt and beat well. Spread over apples. Bake in 350-degree oven 30 to 40 minutes or until golden brown.

Cool to warm, then top with icing made by combining:
1 cup powdered sugar
3 tablespoons frozen orange juice concentrate

APPLE-CHERRY PIE

1½ cups fresh or frozen cherries, chopped
1½ cups chopped apples
¾ cup sugar
3 tablespoons butter

Combine cherries, apples and sugar and pour into an unbaked pie crust. Dot with butter, then top with crust and seal edges. Bake 10 minutes at 450 degrees, then 30 to 40 minutes at 350 degrees.

APPLE CIDER PIE

4 cups sweet apple cider
½ cup sugar
1 cup finely-chopped apples
2 envelopes unflavored gelatin
2 egg whites

Soak gelatin in ¼ cup cider. Bring 2 cups cider to a boil and add soaked gelatin. Stir until dissolved. Add sugar and remaining cider. Chill until syrupy. Pour half of syrupy mixture into a baked pie crust. Sprinkle apples over top and chill until set.

When set, beat other half of gelatin mixture until frothy. Fold in stiffly beaten egg whites and combine well. Pour over apple mixture and chill until well set. Serve cold.

APPLE-COTTAGE CHEESE PIE ·

1½ cups thinly-sliced apples
2 eggs
¾ cup cottage cheese
½ cup sugar
½ cup cream
¼ teaspoon salt
1 teaspoon grated lemon rind
3 tablespoons sugar
½ teaspoon cinnamon
¼ teaspoon nutmeg

Line a 9-inch crust with the sliced apples. In a bowl, beat the eggs slightly, then add the cottage cheese, sugar, cream, salt and lemon rind. Over the apples sprinkle a mixture of the 3 tablespoons sugar, cinnamon and nutmeg, then cover with the cottage cheese mixture. Bake 10 minutes in a 400-degree oven, then 30 minutes more at 350 degrees.

APPLE CRANBERRY PIE

4 tart apples
1¼ cups cranberries
¾ cup sugar
¼ teaspoon cinnamon
¼ teaspoon salt
2 tablespoons butter

Line a pie pan with plain pastry. Peel, core and slice apples thin. Wash and cut cranberries in half. Place one-half the apples in the pastry, top with all the cranberries, then add remaining apples. Sprinkle with a mixture of the sugar, cinnamon and salt. Dot with butter. Cover with top crust, seal edges and bake in 400-degree oven until apples are tender and crust is golden brown.

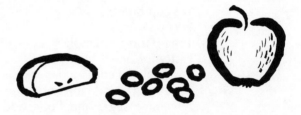

APPLE-CREAM PIE

Peel and core 6 apples and cut into quarters. Simmer in ½ cup water over low heat until apples are tender and almost dry. Rub through a colander and sweeten with ½ cup powdered sugar. Chill.

Meanwhile, beat three egg whites until stiff and season with three tablespoons powdered sugar and ½ teaspoon vanilla. In another bowl, whip one cup heavy cream and sweeten with 4 tablespoons sugar. Into apples gently fold first the egg whites, then the whipped cream. Pour into 2 baked pie crusts and sprinkle with grated nutmeg. Makes 2 pies.

APPLE-CREAM PIE

3 cups finely-chopped apples
1 cup brown sugar
1 cup cream
¼ teaspoon salt
2 tablespoons flour

Combine all ingredients and pour into an unbaked pie crust. Sprinkle top with ¼ teaspoon cinnamon. Bake 15 minutes in a 450-degree oven, then 30 to 40 minutes at 325-degrees.

APPLE CRUMB PIE

6 tart apples
1 cup sugar
1/3 cup butter
¾ cup flour
1 teaspoon cinnamon
Pastry for one 9-inch crust

Peel and core apples and slice into pie shell. Combine ½ cup sugar and cinnamon and sprinkle over apples. Mix remaining sugar and flour, add butter and rub together until it forms crumbs. Sprinkle over the apples. Bake 10 minutes at 450-degrees then reduce temperature to 350 degrees and bake 35 minutes more.

APPLE CRUNCH PIE

Crust:
2¼ cups all-purpose flour
1 teaspoon salt
¾ cup vegetable shortening
¼ cup water

Sift flour and salt into a bowl. Remove 1/3 cup flour and mix with water to make a paste. Cut shortening into remaining flour until pieces are the size of small peas. Add flour paste to the flour-shortening mixture. Mix and shape into a ball. Divide in half. Lightly roll one half of dough in a circle about 12 inches in diameter and ⅛-inch thick. Line pan and trim edges even with edge of pan.

Filling:
6 large tart apples
¾ cup sugar
¼ teaspoon cinnamon
¼ teaspoon salt
1 tablespoon flour
1 teaspoon lemon juice
1 tablespoon vegetable shortening

Peel, core and slice apples. Combine with other ingredients and fill pan. Roll out remaining dough into a 10-inch circle. Make three or four steam vents. Place over apples, fold over lower crust and flute with fingers to seal. Brush top with milk, then sprinkle with topping made by crumbling the following ingredients until crumbly:

Topping:
1 tablespoon vegetable shortening
1 tablespoon sugar
3 tablespoons flour
¼ teaspoon salt
Bake in 400-degree oven 40 to 45 minutes.

APPLE CUSTARD PIE

Peel and core tart apples. Simmer until soft and most of the juice is boiled away. Rub through a colander or put through a blender. In a separate bowl, beat three eggs well. Add 1/3 cup butter, 1/3 cup sugar and ½ teaspoon nutmeg. Fold in cooked apples and pour into an unbaked pie crust. Bake 40 minutes in 350-degree oven or until set.

OR:

6 tart apples
1 cup sugar
1 cup flour
2 tablespoons butter
1 teaspoon cinnamon
1½ cups milk
Pastry for one 9-inch crust

Mix sugar and flour together. Spread evenly in bottom of crust. Peel and core apples, cut into quarters. Place in bottom of unbaked crust, then sprinkle with cinnamon and dot with butter. Pour milk over the mixture and bake in 375-degree oven 50 minutes or until set.

OR:

2 cups applesauce
½ cup sugar
2 eggs, separated
¼ cup melted butter
Pastry for one 9-inch crust

Add sugar, melted butter and egg yolks to applesauce. Mix well. Beat egg whites until they peak, then fold whites into apple mixture. Pour into unbaked crust. Bake 35 minutes in 375-degree oven.

APPLE DAINTY Line a pie tin with flaky pastry and bake in a 350-degree oven until golden brown. While it is cooling, peel, core and quarter 6 tart cooking apples. Cover with a syrup made of 1 cup sugar and 1 cup water. Cook about 20 minutes, or until apples are tender and clear, but have not lost their shape.

Strain out the apples, laying them close together on the baked crust. Continue cooking the syrup until it is thickened. Cool and pour over the apples in the shell. Top with whipped cream and serve.

APPLE DELIGHT

2 tablespoons flour
¾ cup sugar
1 egg, beaten
½ teaspoon vanilla
½ teaspoon salt
½ cup whipping cream
2 cups chopped apples

Combine all ingredients except apples. Beat until smooth. Add apples. Pour into unbaked crust and bake 15 minutes in 450-degree oven. Reduce heat to 400 degrees and bake 30 minutes more, or until center is firm.

Combine the following:

1/3 cup sugar
1 teaspoon cinnamon
1/3 cup flour
¼ cup butter

Mix well and sprinkle over pie. Bake 10 minutes more.

APPLE FLUFF PIE

2 cups applesauce
2 tablespoons lemon juice
1 tablespoon flour
¼ teaspoon salt
2 eggs separated

Combine applesauce, juice, flour, salt and well-beaten egg yolks. Cook in double boiler over hot water until thick and smooth. Fold in stiffly-beaten egg whites and pour into unbaked crust. Bake in 400-degree oven until crust is brown and filling is firm.

13

APPLE MERINGUE PIE

Peel, core and slice 6 tart, juicy apples. Cook with ½ teaspoon grated lemon rind and ½ cup sugar. Mash. Pour into unbaked pie crust and bake in 375-degree oven until done.

Then spread over the top a thick meringue made by beating three egg whites and flavoring with 3 tablespoons powdered sugar and ½ teaspoon vanilla. Pile on pie and brown in a 350-degree oven about 10 minutes.

APPLE-MINCE PIE

3 tart apples, sliced
¼ cup sugar
¼ teaspoon cinnamon
¼ teaspoon nutmeg
¼ teaspoon salt
2 cups mincemeat
3 tablespoons butter

Pour the mincemeat into one side of an unbaked pie crust and the sliced apples on the other. Sprinkle the apples with a mixture of the sugar, salt and spices. Dot both sides with butter. Top with crust, seal edges and bake 30 to 40 minutes at 350-degrees.

APPLE MYSTERY PIE

3 egg yolks, well beaten
1 can sweetened condensed milk
1 cup applesauce
1/3 cup lemon juice
1 tablespoon grated lemon rind
3 egg whites, stiffly beaten

Combine egg yolks, milk, applesauce, juice and rind. Fold in egg whites. Pour into a Graham cracker crust. Top with ½ cup crumbs and chill before serving.

14

APPLE-RAISIN PIE

¾ cup sugar
2 tablespoons flour
¼ teaspoon salt
½ teaspoon cinnamon
4 cups peeled, sliced apples
½ cup seedless raisins
2 tablespoons frozen orange juice concentrate
3 tablespoons butter.

Combine sugar, flour, salt and cinnamon. Mix with apples and raisins and place in unbaked pie crust. Top with orange juice and bits of butter. Cover with top crust and seal edges. Bake 15 minutes in 400-degree oven, then 30 to 40 minutes at 350-degrees.

APPLE-ROSE PIE

Line the bottom of a pie pan with unbaked crust. Put in a layer of sliced apples, then a thin layer (½ cup) of powdered sugar. Alternate rows until pan is filled. Dot with 5 or 6 rose petals and 2 or 3 cloves (or ¼ teaspoon powdered cloves). Top with crust and bake 40 to 45 minutes in 350-degree oven.

APPLE-WALNUT PIE

1 egg, well beaten
1 cup diced apples
1 cup chopped walnuts
2/3 cup sugar
2 tablespoons flour
1 teaspoon baking powder

Sift together dry ingredients. In another bowl, combine egg, apples and nuts. Combine two mixtures well, then spread in an unbaked pie crust and bake 30 to 40 minutes in a 350-degree oven.

APPLE-WINE PIE

Peel and core 6 tart apples. Cut into thick slices. Make a syrup of 1 cup sugar and ½ cup water. Add 3 cloves, ⅛ teaspoon allspice and ½ teaspoon cinnamon and bring to a low boil.

Drop in apple slices, a few at a time, and cook slightly. Then remove to rack to cool and add more slices to cook. When cool, place in unbaked pie crust, sprinkle with flour and dot with butter. Over all pour two ounces sweet wine and top with crust. Bake 40 to 45 minutes in 350-degree oven.

AUNT MAY'S APPLE PIE

6 large tart apples
1 cup sugar
2 tablespoons butter
3 tablespoons water

Peel, core and slice apples. In a saucepan, steam apples in 3 tablespoons water until almost, but not quite, tender. Add ¾ cup sugar and mix gently, so as not to break up apple slices. Pour into an unbaked crust and cover with pastry strips. Over this sprinkle remaining sugar and dot with butter. Bake 10 minutes in 400-degree oven, then 30 minutes at 350-degrees.

CANDIED APPLE PIE

2 cups sliced apples
1½ cups brown sugar
½ cup butter
1 cup flour
1 cup whipped cream

Peel and core apples, then slice into the bottom of a greased 9-inch pie pan. Sprinkle with ½ cup brown sugar.

16

Combine remaining sugar, butter and flour and sprinkle over apples. Bake 45 minutes in 375-degree oven. Serve with whipped cream.

CANNED APPLE PIE

2 cups canned apples
¾ cup sugar
¼ cup flour
½ cup apple juice from can
1 tablespoon butter

Mix sugar and flour in saucepan. Add apple juice to make a smooth paste. Cook over low heat until smooth and thick. Pour apples into an unbaked pie crust and dot with butter. Top with thickened juice. Cover with top crust or lattice strips. Bake in 450-degree oven 10 minutes, then 30 minutes at 350-degrees.

CARAMEL APPLE PIE

¼ cup melted butter
½ cup brown sugar
½ cup chopped pecans
6 tart apples
½ cup granulated sugar
½ teaspoon cinnamon
¼ teaspoon nutmeg
¼ teaspoon salt
2 tablespoons water
3 tablespoons butter

Into an unbaked pie crust brush melted butter and sprinkle brown sugar. Sprinkle with pecans. Over this slice peeled apples and cover with a mixture of the sugar, salt, and spices. Add water and dot with butter. Cover with top crust, seal edges and bake 10 minutes in 450-degree oven, then 30 to 40 minutes at 350-degrees.

DEEP DISH APPLE PIE WITH CANDIED CRUST

Oil a deep dish casserole and fill with sliced tart apples. Meanwhile, combine:

1 cup brown sugar
1 cup flour
¼ teaspoon salt
¼ teaspoon cinnamon
⅛ teaspoon nutmeg
½ cup butter

Work the butter into the dry ingredients until crumbly. Sprinkle the mixture on top of the apples for a top crust. Bake 40 minutes in a 350-degree oven. Serve warm.

DEEP DISH WINDSOR PIE

Peel, core and slice in rounds 6 tart apples. Arrange in 3 layers in a deep earthenware baking dish. Between each

layer sprinkle 1/3 of the following mixture:
1 cup sugar
1 teaspoon cinnamon
2 tablespoons butter
Cover with a batter made by beating 1 egg with ½ cup sugar, 2 tablespoons butter, 1 cup flour and 1 teaspoon baking powder. Spread batter evenly over surface and dot with small pieces of butter. Bake 30 minutes in 400-degree oven.

DRIED APPLE PIE

2 cups dried apples
½ cup sugar
½ teaspoon cinnamon
¼ teaspoon powdered cloves
1 tablespoon butter
1 tablespoon grated orange peel
Soak apples 1 hour, then cook in same water until tender. Remove apples and cook water down until there is ½ cup. Put cooked apples in unbaked pie crust and sprinkle with sugar-spice mixture. Dot with butter and sprinkle with orange peel. Top with crust and bake 40 to 45 minutes in 350-degree oven.

OR:

Soak two cups dried apples in 1 cup water for 1 hour in a brown earthenware pie plate. Cover and bake in a 250-degree oven 4 or 5 hours. Add ¾ cup sugar and stir a little with a spoon. Dot with butter and sprinkle with 2 tablespoons lemon juice. Top with crust and bake at 350-degrees until crust is browned.

OR:

2 cups dried apple slices
2/3 cup sugar
1½ cups warm water
¼ teaspoon powdered cloves
½ teaspoon cinnamon
Pastry for two 9-inch crusts

Soak apples in water, then cook until soft. Run through a blender of mash fine. Add sugar and spices and pour into pie shell. Cover with top crust, seal edges and bake 15 minutes at 425 degrees, then 35 minutes at 375 degrees.

OR:

2 cups dried apples
¾ cup sugar
2 eggs
2 tablespoons cream
¼ cup butter

Cover dried apples with water and simmer 40 minutes, or until apples are tender and water is evaporated. Beat until smooth. In another bowl, cream butter and sugar. Add well-beaten egg yolks, cream and apples. Fold in stiffly-beaten egg whites. Pour into baked pie crust and bake in 400-degree oven until firm.

DRIED APPLE CUSTARD PIE

½ cup dried apples
½ cup sugar
2 eggs, separated
½ teaspoon salt
1½ tablespoons flour
1 teaspoon grated orange rind
1¼ cups milk
Pastry for one 9-inch crust

Soak dried apples in warm water for one hour, then cook until soft. Run through a blender or mash fine. Combine with flour, sugar, salt, flour, orange rind, milk and egg yolks. Mix well, then fold in stiffly-beaten egg whites. Pour into unbaked crust and bake 40 minutes at 375 degrees.

DUTCH APPLE PIE

3 cups sliced apples
1 cup brown sugar
4 tablespoons butter
3 tablespoons flour
1 teaspoon cinnamon
3 tablespoons cream
Pastry for one 9-inch crust

Combine flour, sugar and cinnamon. Mix in butter until crumbled. Put apples in crust and top with crumb mixture. Add cream. Bake 45 minutes at 375 degrees or until apples are soft.

OR:

6 large apples
¼ cup butter
¾ cup sugar
½ teaspoon powdered cinnamon
Pastry for one 9-inch crust

Peel, core and slice apples. Melt butter in a saucepan and add apples. Stir lightly until each slice is coated. Add combined sugar and cinnamon and mix well. Pour mixture into pie crust and bake 15 minutes in 450-degree oven. Then reduce heat to 325 degrees, cover pie with inverted pie pan and continue baking another 30 minutes. Cool before serving.

FAMILY PIE

1 quart sliced apples
1½ cups sugar
2 tablespoons butter
2 teaspoons cinnamon
¼ cup water
Pastry for three 9-inch pie crusts

With one-half the pastry, line sides and bottom of deep baking dish. Combine apple slices, sugar and cinnamon and pour into crust. Dot with butter and add water. Top with remaining crust. Bake 20 minutes in 425-degree oven, then 40 minutes at 375 degrees. Serve with cream. Serves 8.

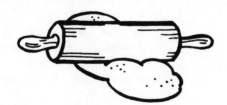

**FRIED APPLE
PIES**

1½ cups all-purpose flour
2 teaspoons baking powder
2 tablespoons sugar
½ teaspoon salt
2 tablespoons shortening
½ cup (about) milk

Combine dry ingredients and cut in shortening to the consistency of cornmeal. Add enough milk to make a stiff dough. Knead a minute or two, then roll out to a sheet ¼-inch thick. Cut in 6-inch rounds and on each round place 1 tablespoon thick, well-seasoned applesauce and a dot of butter.

Fold over round and press edges of dough firmly together to seal. Fry in deep fat until puffed and brown. Drain on absorbent paper. Dust with powdered sugar.

**FRUITED
APPLE PIE**

2 cups dried apples
2 cups dried prunes
2 cups seedless raisins
1 cup light corn syrup
¼ cup vinegar
7½ cups water
1 teaspoon cinnamon
½ teaspoon allspice
½ teaspoon salt
½ teaspoon powdered cloves
½ cup cornstarch

Chop apples and prunes, removing pits. Cover with water. Add raisins and simmer 30 minutes, or until tender. In another saucepan, combine syrup, vinegar, remaining water, spices and salt. Bring to a boil and cook 2 minutes. Add to cooked fruit.

23

Mix well and thicken with cornstarch. Pour into unbaked pie crusts, top with crust and bake in 350-degree oven 30 to 40 minutes, or until brown. Makes two 9 or 10-inch or three 8-inch pies.

GERMAN APPLE PIE

6 tart apples
¾ brown sugar
½ teaspoon cinnamon
butter

Peel, core and slice apples into an unbaked crust. Sprinkle with mixture of sugar and cinnamon and dot with butter. Bake, without a top crust, about 40 minutes in a 350-degree oven.

Meanwhile, combine 1 well-beaten egg, ½ cup heavy cream and 1 tablespoon sugar. Mix well. Remove pie from oven and pour the egg-cream mixture over the top. Return to oven and bake until top custard is set, 15 to 20 minutes.

GREEN APPLE PIE

Peel and core 6 moderately tart, green apples. Pippins, Russets and Greenings are good. Cut into very thin slices and fill a pie crust. Sprinkle over them ½ cup brown sugar mixed with 1 teaspoon cinnamon.

Dot with butter and sprinkle with 2 or 3 tablespoons apple cider. Top with the upper crust and flute edges to seal. Bake in a 350-degree oven 40 minutes, or until brown.

24

HONEY APPLE PIE

6 tart apples
1/3 cup honey
½ teaspoon salt
¼ teaspoon cinnamon
2 tablespoons butter

Slice apples into unbaked pie crust. Sprinkle with salt and cinnamon, add the honey and dot with butter. Top with crust, seal and bake 40 minutes in 350-degree oven.

JELLED HONEY APPLE PIE

2 cups dried apples
3 cups water
1/3 cup honey
1/3 cup sugar
1 tablespoon unflavored gelatin
2 tablespoons cold water
1 cup heavy cream, whipped
¼ teaspoon salt
4 drops almond flavoring
1 baked pie crust

Cover apples with water and cook gently for 30 minutes. Five minutes before removing from heat, add honey and sugar. Mash apples to make a sauce. Sprinkle gelatin over cold water in a cup, then add to hot pulp.

Reheat to thoroughly dissolve gelatin. Chill. Fold in whipped cream, salt and flavoring. Pour into baked pie crust and chill before serving.

**LOW CAL
APPLE PIE**

1½ cups all-purpose flour
½ teaspoon baking powder
2 teaspoons soda
½ teaspoon salt
1 tablespoon shortening
½ cup sour milk or buttermilk
2 cups sliced apples.

Mix together the dry ingredients, then cut in the shortening. Mix in enough sour milk to make a stiff dough. Roll out ¼-inch thick to a circle about four inches larger than the pie pan. Center rolled dough on pie pan, but do not trim.

Pour in cooked, unsweetened apples. Sprinkle with cinnamon and fold dough over top, leaving center open. Bake 30 minutes in 350-degree oven, or until brown.

**MAPLE-CIDER
PIE**

1/3 cup rich cider
1/3 cup grated maple sugar
2 eggs, beaten
1 tablespoon butter
¾ cup seedless raisins
½ teaspoon grated nutmeg

Heat sugar and cider until sugar dissolves. Add beaten eggs and cook until thickened. Add butter, raisins and nutmeg. Pour into an unbaked crust, cover with top crust and bake 10 minutes at 450 degrees, then 30 minutes at 400 degrees.

MARSHMALLOW APPLE PIE

6 tart apples
1 tablespoon butter
¼ teaspoon salt
½ cup sugar
½ teaspoon nutmeg
12 marshmallows, cut in half

Line a pie pan with unbaked crust, then fill with sliced apples. Combine sugar, salt and nutmeg, then sprinkle over apples. Dot with butter. Bake in a 425-degree oven until the crust is brown and the apples are tender.

Remove from oven and cover apples with marshmallows, cut sides down. Return to 325-degree oven until marshmallows are melted and browned. Serve warm.

MOCK MINCEMEAT PIE

8 large tart apples
½ cup seedless raisins
½ cup seedless dried currants
1½ cups brown sugar
½ cup cider
½ cup vinegar
½ lemon, juice and grated peel
½ teaspoon grated orange peel
¼ teaspoon salt
¼ teaspoon nutmeg
¼ teaspoon allspice
½ teaspoon cinnamon

Core and quarter unpeeled apples. Put through food chopper with raisins and currants. Combine all ingredients in large pan. Simmer two hours over low heat, stirring frequently to keep from sticking. Enough for two pies.

27

OLD VIRGINIA APPLE PIE

2 baked pie crusts
4 cups cold applesauce
whipped cream

Fill each crust with 2 cups applesauce, then stack one crust on the other. Cover with whipped cream and cut in sections to serve.

OPEN-FACED APPLE PIE

7 medium apples
¾ cup sugar
2 tablespoons butter
1/3 cup flour
¼ cup water
2 tablespoons lemon juice
Pastry for one 9-inch crust

Mix together sugar, butter and flour. Sprinkle half the mixture in the bottom of unbaked crust. Peel and core apples and cut in halves. Place, cut side down, in crust. Cover with remainder of crumb mixture. Mix together water and lemon juice and pour over apples. Bake 15 minutes in 425-degree oven, then 35 minutes at 375-degrees.

ORANGE-APPLE PIE

6 tart apples
1 cup brown sugar
1½ tablespoons tapioca
Grated rind of 1 orange
¼ teaspoon salt
¼ cup orange juice
2 tablespoons butter

Line a 9-inch pie pan with unbaked pie crust. Peel, core

and thinly slice apples and place half of them in crust. Combine sugar, tapioca, grated rind and salt. Pour over apples and add orange juice. Dot with butter. Add remaining apples and cover with top crust. Brush lightly with milk for better browning. Bake 10 minutes at 450-degrees, then 30 minutes at 350 degrees.

PEANUT BUTTER APPLE PIE

Crust:
    2 cups all-purpose flour
    2½ teaspoons baking powder
    ½ teaspoon salt
    ¼ cup peanut butter
    ¼ cup butter
    ¾ cup milk
    Mix flour, baking powder and salt. Cut in peanut butter and butter until crumbs are like coarse cornmeal. Stir in milk and stir with a fork until the dough cleans the bowl. Place dough on a heavily floured surface and knead to a smooth ball. Divide in half and roll one piece to the size of a pie pan. Place on pan and trim to fit.

Filling:
    6 cooking apples, peeled, cored and sliced
    ½ cup raisins
    6 tablespoons sugar
    Fill crust with filling and top with remaining crust, fluting edges to seal. Bake in 375-degree oven 40 to 45 minutes, or until apples are tender and crust is brown. Serve warm, topped with sauce.

Sauce:
3 tablespoons cornstarch
1 can (6 ounces) frozen lemonade, undiluted
1½ cups water
2 tablespoons butter
Simmer over low heat until sauce bubbles and thickens.

**PINEAPPLE
APPLE PIE**

2 cups thinly slice apples
½ cup sugar
¼ teaspoon salt
1 tablespoon flour
Butter
½ cup crushed pineapple, drained
¼ cup sugar
1 tablespoon lemon juice
2 egg whites
2 tablespoons sugar

Line a 9-inch pie pan with crust. Pour in apples. Combine sugar, salt and flour and pour over apples. Dot with butter. Bake, uncovered, in 350-degree oven about 40 minutes, or until apples are tender.

Meanwhile, combine the pineapple, sugar and lemon juice and heat to boiling. Boil 1 minute, then spread over top of pie. Cover with meringue made with the 2 egg whites and 2 tablespoons sugar. Brown meringue in 400-degree oven.

**QUICK
APPLE PIE**

6 tart apples
1 cup sugar
1 teaspoon cinnamon
¼ teaspoon salt
3 tablespoons milk
2 tablespoons butter
1½ cups homemade pastry mix (Page 45)

Slice peeled apples into empty pie pan. Pour over them a mixture of the sugar, cinnamon and salt. Add milk and dot with butter. Sprinkle the pastry mix over the top, patting down to smooth.

Bake in 350-degree oven 30 to 40 minutes, or until apples are tender and top crust is brown.

**RED HOT
APPLE PIE**

6 tart apples, peeled and sliced
1/3 cup sugar
¼ teaspoon salt
3 tablespoons flour
¼ cup water
2 tablespoons red cinnamon candies
3 tablespoons butter

Slice apples into an unbaked pie crust. In a saucepan, heat water to boiling, add candies and stir to dissolve. Add sugar, salt and flour and cook over low heat until thickened. Pour over sliced apples and dot with butter. Cover with lattice crust and bake 10 minutes at 450 degrees, then 30 to 40 minutes at 350 degrees.

31

SOUR CREAM APPLE PIE

2 cups apples, finely chopped
2 tablespoons flour
½ teaspoon vanilla
1 cup sour cream
¾ cup sugar
1 egg
¼ teaspoon salt

Combine dry ingredients in a bowl. Add egg, cream, and vanilla and beat until smooth. Add apples and mix well. Pour into unbaked pie crust and bake at 450-degrees for 10 minutes, then 15 minutes at 350 degrees.

Remove from oven and top with a mixture of:
1/3 cup flour
1/3 cup sugar
1 teaspoon cinnamon
¼ cup butter

Return to oven and bake 15 minutes more.

APPLES WRAPPED IN CRUST

No collection of apple pie recipes would be complete without including some of the many other good things that can be made of crust and apples and spice. Here are a few of the favorites:

APPLE DUMPLINGS

6 tart apples
½ cup sugar
½ teaspoon cinnamon
2 tablespoons butter
Pastry for two-crust pie

Roll out pastry to ¼-inch thick and cut into six 6-inch squares. Peel and core apples, leaving whole. Place an apple on each square. Combine the sugar and cinnamon and fill center of each apple. Moisten edges of pastry and bring all four corners to the center. Seal. Place in a greased baking dish and refrigerate while you make Cider Sauce.

Sauce:
1 cup sweet apple cider
½ cup sugar
½ teaspoon cinnamon
3 tablespoons butter

Bring to a boil and simmer 2 minutes. Pour, boiling hot, into baking dish around dumplings. Bake 10 minutes at 450 degrees, then 30 minutes at 350 degrees. Serve warm.

PEANUT BUTTER JELLY DUMPLINGS

Crust:
    4 cups all-purpose flour
    5 teaspoons baking powder
    1 teaspoon salt
    ½ cup butter
    1½ cups milk
Mix flour, baking powder and salt. Cut in butter until crumbs are like coarse cornmeal. Add milk and stir with a fork until dough comes away from the bowl. Place on a floured board and knead a few times to make a ball. Roll out to an oblong 12 by 18 inches. Cut into six 6-inch squares.

Filling:
    6 tart apples, peeled and cored, whole
    1/3 cup peanut butter
    1/3 cup jelly or marmalade
Place an apple in the center of each square. In each apple place a spoonful of jelly, then of peanut butter. Bring up all four corners of dough, moisten edges and seal. Place in a baking dish and bake in a 350-degree oven until apples are tender and crust is browned. Meanwhile make sauce.

Sauce:
    3 tablespoons cornstarch
    1 can frozen lemonade concentrate
    1½ cups water
    2 tablespoons butter
Dissolve cornstarch in water and cook until very thick. Add lemonade and butter and serve hot over hot dumplings.

APPLE PAN DOWDY

6 medium apples
3 tablespoons brown sugar
3 tablespoons molasses
¼ teaspoon grated nutmeg
½ teaspoon powdered cinnamon
½ teaspoon salt
½ cup hot water
Biscuit dough made with 1 cup flour

Peel, core and slice apples. Place in a 1½-quart baking dish. Sprinkle with sugar, molasses, spices and salt. Sprinkle with hot water. Bake 20 minutes, or until tender.

Spread biscuit dough evenly over the top and bake 15 to 20 minutes longer, or until crust is lightly browned. Serve hot or cold with cream.

APPLE ROLY POLY

2 cups cooked apples
¼ cup sugar
½ teaspoon grated lemon peel
1/3 cup butter
Biscuit dough made with 2 cups flour
1 egg white
Cream

Roll biscuit dough 1/3-inch thick. Beat egg white slightly and brush over dough. Spread dough with mixture of apples, sugar, lemon peel and butter, then roll up like a jelly roll.

Cut into one-inch slices and place slices in greased baking pan. Bake 25 minutes in 400-degree oven. Serve warm with cream.

APPLE TARTS

2 cups dried apples
½ cup sugar
1½ cups warm water
Pastry for two 9-inch crusts

Soak dried apples in warm water for 1 hour. Then cook in same water until tender. Add sugar. Drain and cool. Roll pastry and cut into 4-inch squares. Put filling in center of each square. Moisten edges and bring corners up and press together. Bake 20 minutes in 400-degree oven or until golden brown.

APPLE TURNOVERS

2 cups dried apples
1½ cups warm water
½ cup sugar
2 tablespoons butter
1 teaspoon cinnamon
Pastry for two 9-inch crusts

Soak apples in water, then cook in same water until apples are tender and most of the water has evaporated. Add sugar, butter and cinnamon. Mix well. Roll out pastry and cut into 5-inch circles. Place three tablespoonfuls of apple mixture on each circle, then fold over dough and seal edges. Press edges securely.

Fry in deep fat at 375 degrees for about 5 minutes, or until golden brown. Turnovers also may be baked in 350-degree oven for 25 minutes.

APPLE STRUDEL

1½ cups flour
¼ teaspoon salt
1 egg, beaten
1/3 cup lukewarm water
2 tablespoons melted butter
2 pounds tart apples
1½ cups seedless raisins
1½ teaspoons powdered cinnamon
1 cup shredded, blanched almonds
1 cup sugar
5 tablespoons melted butter

Combine flour and salt in mixing bowl and add egg mixed with water. Blend into a dough and knead until elastic. Dust lightly with flour, cover with a warm bowl and let stand 30 minutes. Then work the 2 tablespoons butter into the dough and spread a clean cloth on a working surface. Dust cloth with flour and place dough in the middle. Working with the hands, gently pull and stretch the dough until it is thin as paper. It should stretch to a square 18 inches each way.

Meanwhile, grease two large baking sheets and peel, core and chop apples. Combine with raisins, cinnamon, almonds, sugar and 5 tablespoons melted butter. Mix well. Spread the stretched dough with the apple mixture, then roll tightly into one large roll. Cut into two-inch pieces and place on baking sheets.

Bake 30 minutes in 400-degree oven, then reduce heat to 350 degrees and bake 10 minutes longer, or until lightly browned. Serve warm, sprinkled with powdered sugar.

THE CRUSTS

Pastry is a rich dough often used for pie crust. The basic ingredients are flour, fat and liquid. The usual ratio is one part fat to three parts flour.

But these ingredients may be varied almost infinitely. The flour may be all-purpose, whole wheat or a mixture of wheat and soy, rye or rice flours, or even special pastry flour grinds.

The fat may be lard, butter, margarine or vegetable shortening or oil. For meat pies, beef suet or chicken fat is appropriate.

Many good cooks prefer lard, which they say makes the flakiest crust. Pastry made with vegetable shortening is the easiest to work with. Butter or margarine give crusts a good flavor, but are best combined with lard or vegetable shortening. And finally, vegetable oil makes a rather brittle crust but is the most healthful, especially if corn or safflower oil is used, because of the lower cholesterol content.

Except for hot water pastries, fat should be cold and firm when it is added to the flour. Mix the fat and flour with a pastry blender or two knives. Cut the fat into the flour well before adding the liquid.

The amount of liquid must be carefully measured, for too much liquid makes a crust tough. Too little makes pastry hard to handle. A safe rule is 2 to 4 tablespoons of liquid to each cup of flour.

We begin with six basic recipes for pastry and a recipe for homemade pastry mix.

But not all pie crust is pastry. Pie crust can be made of almost anything you like, in an almost endless list of variations — 35 different kinds of crusts which are baked before or after filling and 8 crusts which are used without baking.

Use them to give delicious variety to your apple pies.

BAKED CRUSTS

The following crusts are baked before filling for pies such as Old Virginia, or are filled and then baked, as in Apple Mince. The pastries are suitable for one- or two-crust pies. Others such as Graham Cracker, which are pressed into the pan, are used only for bottom crusts.

PLAIN PASTRY

2 cups all-purpose flour
½ teaspoon salt
2/3 cup fat
5 to 6 tablespoons ice water

Sift flour and salt into a mixing bowl. Work in fat with a pastry blender, two knives or the fingers, until the mixture has the consistency of very coarse meal or small peas. Add the water, sprinkling it over the dry ingredients. Stir with a fork until the dough forms a ball.

Wrap in waxed paper and chill one or two hours in the refrigerator. Makes two 9-inch bottom crusts or one bottom crust and one top crust for one 9-inch pie.

To make a baked pie shell for such recipes as Apple-Cream Pie or Old Virginia Apple Pie, roll out one-half the dough to a 10-inch circle and line sides and bottom of a 9-inch pan. Trim edges to within ½ inch of the pan, folding under surplus and crimping edges with fingers. Prick crust all over with a fork and bake in a 350-degree oven 15 to 20 minutes, until brown.

To make a two-crust pie, line a 9-inch pie pan with one-half the dough and trim edges close to the pan. Roll remaining dough to a 10-inch circle. Fill pie shell and top with crust which has had one-inch steam slits cut in the center. Trim edges of top crust to within ½ inch of the pan, fold under bottom crust edge and crimp to seal the two crusts together. Bake according to the individual recipe or 10 minutes in a 450-degree oven, then at 350 degrees until fruit is tender and crust is browned, usually about 30 minutes more.

FLAKY PASTRY

3 cups all-purpose flour
1 teaspoon salt
½ cup butter
¾ cup ice water
½ cup lard

Sift the flour and salt together. Add the butter and lard and cut with two knives until no piece is larger than a pea. Sprinkle with ice water and mix with a fork until a soft dough is formed. Place on a floured board, dust with flour and roll with a rolling pin until the dough becomes an oblong sheet ½ inch thick.

Fold both ends toward the middle, making the dough three layers thick. Lift the dough from the board with a knife. Lightly dust the board under it with flour, dust the top of the dough with flour and roll again.

Once again fold over both ends to form a three-layer dough. Repeat. Chill 1 hour before rolling to fill pie pans. Makes three crusts.

RICH PASTRY

2 cups all-purpose flour
½ teaspoon salt
1/3 teaspoon baking powder
1/3 cup butter
1/3 cup lard

Sift together flour, salt and baking powder. Cut in 1/3 cup lard to the consistency of coarse meal, then sprinkle with water and stir with fork to form a dough. Immediately roll out on floured board into a large rectangle.

Dot with one-third of the butter and roll up like a jelly roll. Pat down and roll out again with rolling pin. Dot with another one-third of the butter, roll up and repeat, using the last of the butter.

Wrap in waxed paper and chill before rolling. Makes two 9-inch crusts.

OIL PASTRY

2 cups all-purpose flour
½ teaspoon salt
1 teaspoon baking powder
½ cup salad oil (preferably corn or safflower)
6 tablespoons ice water

Combine flour, salt and baking powder in large mixing bowl. In another bowl, whip oil with water to blend as much as possible. All at once, combine the two mixtures and stir with a fork to form a dough. Divide dough into two portions. Roll out immediately, without chilling. Makes two 8-inch crusts.

WHOLE WHEAT PASTRY

1 cup whole wheat flour
1 cup all-purpose flour
½ teaspoon salt
2/3 cup lard or shortening
4 to 5 tablespoons cold milk

Mix flours and salt. Cut in lard or shortening with pastry blender or hands. Add milk and stir with a fork to form a soft dough. Chill overnight in refrigerator. Makes two 8-inch crusts.

PASTRY MIX

If you serve pie often, you may want to have an "instant pastry mix" on hand to which you can simply add milk or ice water and roll out. The lard or shortening can be cut in by using the electric mixer.

8 cups all-purpose flour
2 teaspoons salt
2 cups lard or shortening

Sift together flour and salt and put in mixer bowl. Cut in shortening with mixer on low speed. Put in an air-tight container and store in refrigerator.

To make a one-crust pie, take out 1½ cups. In a separate bowl, blend 3 tablespoons water with 3 tablespoons flour to form a paste. Stir into pastry mix and roll out.

To make a two-crust pie take out 2 cups of mixture and add a paste made by blending ¼ cup water and ¼ cup flour.

LYDIA'S PIE CRUST MIX

9 pounds all-purpose flour
1 cup cornstarch
1 tablespoon baking powder
2 cups powdered sugar
1 tablespoon salt
4 pounds lard

Mix dry ingredients thoroughly, then cut in lard, working in well until mixture is the consistency of cornmeal. Store, tightly sealed, in a cool, dry place.

To use, measure 1½ cups of mix for each crust. Moisten with mixture (half and half) of vinegar and water.

PUFF PASTRIES

The most elegant of the pastry crusts, puff pastry, is light and flaky, made up of several delicate layers. It is delicious and dainty, the aristocrat of the pastry family.

It is difficult and time consuming to make. But to our great-grandmothers, making a "puff paste" was the final exam of a really good cook.

Here is an old recipe. When you try it, do it on a day when you have plenty of patience and time. It takes about four hours in all.

PUFF PASTRY

1¾ cups flour
¾ teaspoon salt
1 cup butter
½ cup plus 2 tablespoons ice water

Sift the flour, measure it and sift again with the salt. Divide the butter in three equal parts. Work one-third into the flour until the mixture is the texture of coarse cornmeal. Add the ice water, stirring with a fork, until the dough is moist enough to shape into a ball. Turn out on a lightly floured board and knead about 5 minutes. Wrap in waxed paper and chill at least 1 hour in the refrigerator.

Beat the remaining butter until creamy, then chill it.

Divide the dough in two parts and roll each into an oblong sheet ⅛ inch thick. Spread with half the chilled butter and place the other oblong sheet of dough on top of the buttered dough.

Press the edges together, and fold one end over the other, in half. Press the edges together, then fold again in the opposite direction. Chill 1 hour.

Roll on a lightly-floured board and spread with the remaining butter. Fold opposite edges together, press down, then fold again in the opposite directions. Chill again for 1 hour.

When ready to use, roll the chilled dough out to ¼-inch thickness and cut for tarts or patty shells. Perforate the pastry with the tines of a fork, then chill again before baking. Bake on baking sheet or small pie tins rinsed with cold water.

Bake in 450-degree oven 5 to 8 minutes or until it rises and browns delicately. Then reduce the heat to 350 degrees and bake 15 minutes more. Turn several times. Makes one to two dozen fancy pastries or one two-crust pie.

BUTTERMILK PASTRY

2 cups all-purpose flour
½ teaspoon salt
¼ teaspoon soda
2/3 cup shortening
5 to 6 tablespoons cold buttermilk

Sift together flour, salt and soda. Cut in shortening until mixture is the consistency of coarse meal. Sprinkle with buttermilk and stir with a fork to form a dough. Chill before rolling out. Makes two 9-inch crusts.

CHEDDAR CHEESE CRUST

2 cups all-purpose flour
½ teaspoon salt
2/3 cup shortening
5 to 6 tablespoons milk
1 cup grated cheddar cheese

Mix flour and salt, then cut in shortening to the size of a coarse meal. Stir in milk and mix with a fork to form a dough. Roll out on floured board and sprinkle with grated cheese.

Roll up like a jelly roll and fold both ends toward center. Fold in half again. Now roll out again and cut for crusts. Makes two 9-inch crusts.

POTATO CRUST

Cook 3 large potatoes until tender. Mash while hot. Add 2 cups all-purpose flour and 1 teaspoon salt. Mix well. Cut in 1 cup butter and roll out on well-floured board. Knead dough and roll out.

CORNFLAKE CRUST

4 cups cornflakes (about 1½ cups when crushed)
1/3 cup softened butter or margarine
2 tablespoons sugar
⅛ teaspoon grated nutmeg

Combine all ingredients and press firmly against bottom and sides of 7-inch pie pan. Chill at least an hour, then use without baking or bake 10 minutes in a 350-degree oven. Cool before filling.

CORNMEAL CRUST

½ cup cornmeal
¾ cup vanilla wafer crumbs
1/3 cup salad oil

Blend ingredients. Press into 9-inch pie pan. Chill, then bake before filling. Makes one 9-inch crust.

COTTAGE CHEESE CRUST

¼ pound cottage cheese
1 cup salad oil
1 cup whole wheat flour (about)

Blend cottage cheese and oil in blender. Stir in enough flour to make a firm dough. Chill before rolling. Bake in a 350-degree oven 10 to 12 minutes, or until brown. Makes one 9-inch crust.

CREAM CHEESE CRUST

2 cups flour
½ teaspoon salt
1/3 cup fat
1/3 cup cream cheese
5 to 6 tablespoons cold milk

Sift together flour and salt and cut in fat and cream cheese. Blend until it is the consistency of coarse meal, then sprinkle with cold milk. Stir with a fork to form a dough, then wrap in waxed paper and chill one hour or overnight before rolling. Makes two crusts.

EASY-DOES IT CRUST

2 cups all-purpose flour
1 cup shortening, room temperature
½ cup hot water
½ teaspoon salt
¼ teaspoon baking powder

Pour hot water over shortening and stir until melted. Add 2 tablespoons flour and stir well. Mix remaining flour with salt and baking powder and add, a little at a time, until all is well mixed. Roll on lightly floured board. Makes 4 small crusts.

EGG PASTRY

2 cups all-purpose flour
½ teaspoon salt
2/3 cup shortening
2 tablespoons ice water
1 tablespoon lemon juice
1 egg yolk

Sift together flour and salt and cut in shortening, blending until it is the consistency of coarse cornmeal. In a cup combine ice water, lemon juice and egg yolk. Beat thoroughly, then add to flour-shortening mixture. Stir with a fork to form a dough. Chill before rolling. Makes two 9-inch crusts.

FRUIT PIE CRUST

1 cup shortening
3 cups all-purpose flour
1 teaspoon salt
1 egg
1 tablespoon vinegar
6 tablespoons cold water

Combine flour and salt and cut in shortening until the mixture is the consistency of cornmeal. In a small bowl, beat together the egg, vinegar and water until well mixed. Combine with dry mixture and form into a dough. Knead lightly. Dough will be sticky. Chill 1 hour, then roll out. Will make 4 crusts.

GRAHAM CRACKER CRUST

1¼ cups finely crushed Graham cracker crumbs
3 tablespoons sugar
½ cup butter or margarine
1 tablespoon water

Combine crumbs and sugar, then work in softened butter or margarine. Add water, using just enough to hold mixture together. Press firmly on bottom and sides of a 9-inch pie pan. Bake 10 minutes in 350-degree oven. Cool before filling. Makes one 9-inch shell.

OR:

1 cup Graham cracker crumbs
3 tablespoons brown sugar
¼ cup melted butter

Mix ingredients thoroughly, then press firmly in bottom and around sides of a 9-inch pie pan. Bake 5 to 8 minutes in 350-degree oven. Cool.

GRANOLA CRUST

½ cup granola
milk

Add sufficient milk to moisten granola slightly. Immediately press into 9-inch pie pan. Bake 10 minutes in 350-degree oven. Makes one crust.

HEALTH PIE CRUST

2/3 cup whole wheat bread crumbs
¼ cup wheat germ
¼ cup powdered milk
½ teaspoon cinnamon
1/3 cup melted butter
1 tablespoon molasses

To make crumbs, toast bread slices in a 300-degree oven until brown and crisp. Then run through a blender or meat grinder to make fine crumbs.

Measure 2/3 cup. Combine with wheat germ,

powdered milk and cinnamon and add melted butter. Mix well, then blend in molasses. Press against sides and bottom of a well-greased 9-inch pie pan. Bake 10 minutes in a 300-degree oven.

HOT WATER PASTRY

¾ cup shortening or lard, softened
¼ cup boiling water
1 tablespoon milk
2 cups all-purpose flour
½ teaspoon salt

Place shortening or lard (do not use butter, margarine or salad oil), boiling water and milk in a mixing bowl. Beat until mixture is smooth and thick. Add combined dry ingredients and stir quickly until dough rounds up in the center and no longer sticks to the sides of the bowl. Enough for two crusts.

LEMON PASTRY

2 cups all-purpose flour
½ teaspoon salt
2/3 cup shortening
1 teaspoon grated lemon peel
3 tablespoons ice water
3 tablespoons lemon juice

Sift together flour and salt. Cut in shortening and lemon peel, working with a pastry blender or the fingers until it is the consistency of coarse meal. Sprinkle with a mixture of lemon juice and water and stir with a fork to make a stiff dough. Chill in refrigerator before rolling.

NEVER-FAIL PIE CRUST

1 cup shortening
3 cups flour
¼ teaspoon salt
1 egg
1 teaspoon lemon juice
5 tablespoons cold water

Combine flour and salt in a bowl and cut in shortening to the consistency of coarse cornmeal. In a separate bowl, beat egg well, then add lemon juice and water. Add liquid to dry ingredients and stir to form a dough. Makes 3 crusts.

NUT CRUST

1¾ cups whole wheat flour
½ teaspoon salt
½ cup ground nut meats
1/3 cup salad oil
1 tablespoon honey
¼ cup ice water

Mix flour, salt and ground nut meats. Stir in oil and honey. Blend. Add enough water to make a stiff dough. Roll out. Makes two 9-inch crusts.

OR:

1½ cups all-purpose flour
½ cup ground nut meats
¾ teaspoon salt
2/3 cup shortening
5 to 6 tablespoons ice water

Sift together flour, salt and ground nut meats. Cut in shortening until consistency of coarse meal, then sprinkle with ice water and stir with fork to form dough. Chill. Makes two 9-inch crusts.

OATMEAL PIE CRUST

1 cup quick-cooking oats
1/3 cup all-purpose flour
1/3 cup brown sugar
½ teaspoon salt
1/3 cup butter

Combine dry ingredients, mixing well. Cut in butter until crumbly and press firmly on the bottom and sides of a 9-inch pie pan. Bake 15 minutes in a 375-degree oven. Cool, then fill.

ORANGE PASTRY

2 cups all-purpose flour
½ teaspoon salt
2/3 cup shortening
1 teaspoon grated orange peel
5 to 6 tablespoons orange juice

Sift together flour and salt. Cut in shortening and orange peel, working with pastry blender or fingers until mixture is the consistency of coarse cornmeal. Sprinkle with orange juice and stir with fork to form a dough. Chill overnight. Makes two 9-inch crusts.

PASTRY FOR CHICKEN PIES

2 cups all-purpose flour
½ teaspoon salt
½ teaspoon baking powder
½ cup chilled chicken fat
5 to 6 tablespoons ice water

Sift together flour, salt and baking powder. Cut in chicken fat, working quickly to keep it from melting. Sprinkle with ice water and stir with a fork to form a dough. Chill overnight before rolling. Makes two 9-inch crusts.

PASTRY FOR MEAT OR VEGETABLE PIES

2 cups all-purpose flour
½ teaspoon salt
¼ teaspoon baking powder
¼ cup lard
¼ cup beef suet
5 to 6 tablespoons ice water

Sift together flour, salt and baking powder. Cut in lard and suet, working until the mixture is the consistency of coarse meal. Sprinkle with ice water and stir with fork to form a dough. Chill. Makes two 9-inch crusts.

PEANUT FLOUR CRUST

½ cup peanut flour
1½ cups all-purpose flour
2/3 cup shortening
½ teaspoon salt
Ice water

Combine flours and salt. Cut in shortening to the consistency of coarse meal. Sprinkle with enough ice water to form a soft dough. Divide in half. Roll out and fit into pie pan, then chill before baking. Makes two 9-inch crusts.

RYE-POPPY SEED CRUST

2 cups rye flour
½ teaspoon salt
1 tablespoon poppy seeds
½ cup salad oil
Ice water

Combine flour, salt and seeds. Stir in oil with a fork, adding a few drops of water at a time to form a dough. Press into 9-inch pie pan. Chill and bake. Makes one 9-inch crust.

RYE-RICE CRUST

¾ cup rye flour
¾ cup rice flour
½ teaspoon salt
½ cup oil
4 tablespoons ice water

Combine flours and salt. Stir in oil and add enough water to make a firm dough. Roll out. Makes two 9-inch crusts.

SOY CRUST

¼ cup soy flour
1¼ cups all-purpose flour
¾ teaspoon salt
½ cup shortening
3 tablespoons ice water

Combine flours and salt. Cut in shortening and mix with fingers until the consistency of coarse cornmeal. Blend in water and stir with fork to form a dough. Knead a minute or two, then roll to fit pie pan. Makes one bottom crust.

SOY-CHEESE CRUST

1 cup soy flour
1 teaspoon salt
1 tablespoon nutritional yeast
2 egg yolks, beaten
3 tablespoons milk
5 tablespoons cheddar cheese, grated

Combine flour, salt and yeast. Blend egg yolks with milk. Gradually add liquids to sifted ingredients. Work in cheese. Chill. Roll dough thin. Makes one 9-inch crust.

TOASTED SOYBEAN CRUST

½ cup salad oil
1 tablespoon hot water
2 tablespoons buttermilk
1½ tablespoons honey
1¼ cups whole wheat flour
½ teaspoon salt
1/3 cups ground toasted soybeans

Mix first four ingredients, then sprinkle with combined flour and salt. Blend into a dough and roll out two circles and line two pie pans. Press ground soybeans into pastry, prick with fork and bake 10 to 15 minutes in a 400-degree oven. Makes two 9-inch crusts.

WHOLE WHEAT RYE CRUST

1½ cups whole wheat flour
1 cup rye flour
½ teaspoon salt
6 tablespoons oil
2½ tablespoons ice water

Mix flours and salt. Stir in oil and water, mixed, then combine to make a stiff dough. Chill before rolling. Makes two 9-inch crusts.

WHOLE WHEAT
PASTRY

1½ cups whole wheat flour
½ teaspoon salt
½ cup salad oil
3 tablespoons ice water
    Sift together flour and salt. Blend in oil. Add water. Mix thoroughly with a fork until it forms a dough. Divide in half and roll out each half ⅛-inch thick on floured board. Makes two 9-inch crusts.

OR:

½ cup boiling water
1 cup salad oil
2 cups whole wheat flour
¾ teaspoon salt
    Pour boiling water over oil. Blend. Sift flour and salt. Stir into liquid. Mix thoroughly. Chill 30 minutes before rolling out. Makes two 9-inch crusts.

WHOLE WHEAT
RAISIN CRUST

1½ cups whole wheat flour
½ cup raisins, chopped
3 teaspoons salad oil
¼ teaspoon cinnamon
    Blend ingredients. Press into 9-inch pie pan. Chill and bake. Makes one 9-inch crust.

WHOLE WHEAT
SOY CRUST

2 cups whole wheat flour
½ cup soy flour
½ teaspoon salt
6 tablespoons oil
2½ tablespoons ice water

Mix flours and salt. Stir in oil. Add enough water to make a stiff dough. Chill. Makes two 9-inch crusts.

YEAST CRUST

1 teaspoon dry yeast
⅛ cup lukewarm water
1 egg, beaten
1½ tablespoons salad oil
1/3 cup milk
¾ teaspoon salt
1½ cups whole wheat flour

Soften yeast in warm water. Blend egg, oil, milk and salt. Heat to lukewarm. Combine with softened yeast. Stir in flour and mix well. Turn into oiled bowl. Cover and set in a warm place to rise 45 minutes. Turn onto floured board and knead 5 minutes. Divide in half and roll thin. Makes two 9-inch crusts.

UNBAKED PIE CRUSTS

These pie crusts are filled with cooked fillings and are used without baking. They are used only as bottom crusts for one-crust pies.

BRAZIL NUT CRUST

1½ cups Brazil nuts, ground
1 tablespoon salad oil
1 tablespoon honey
    Blend all ingredients. Press into one 9-inch pie pan. Chill.

COCONUT CRUST

1 cup shredded coconut
½ cup wheat germ
1 tablespoon honey
1 tablespoon oil
    Combine ingredients. Press into one 9-inch pie pan. Chill.

COOKIE CRUST

1 cup vanilla wafers
¼ cup softened butter
2 tablespoons sugar
    Blend ingredients. Press into one 8-inch pie pan. Chill before filling.

GRAHAM CRACKER CRUST

1½ cups Graham cracker crumbs
1/3 cup powdered sugar
½ cup softened butter
1 teaspoon flour
 Blend ingredients. Press into 9-inch pie pan. Chill before filling.

NUT-CRUMB CRUST

½ cup ground nut meats
½ cup chocolate cookie crumbs
1/3 cup salad oil
 Combine ingredients. Press into one 9-inch pie pan. Chill.

WHEAT GERM CRUST

½ cup wheat germ
¾ cup Graham cracker crumbs
1/3 cup salad oil
1 tablespoon honey
    Combine ingredients. Press into one 9-inch pie pan. Chill.

**WHOLE WHEAT
BREAD CRUST**

1½ cups dry homemade whole wheat bread crumbs
1 tablespoon honey
½ cup salad oil
    Combine ingredients. Press into one 9-inch pie pan. Chill.

ZWIEBACK CRUST

1 cup Zwieback crumbs
1/3 cup salad oil
¼ teaspoon lemon juice
    Combine ingredients. Press into one 9-inch pie pan. Chill.

PASTRY TIPS

TO SEAL BOTTOM CRUST To keep fruit juices from making the bottom crust soggy, brush the crust well with beaten egg before filling with the fruit.

TO MAKE A LATTICE TOP Cut top crust into ½-inch strips about 10 inches long. Lay the strips across the filled pie, alternating rows for a woven effect. Lay one strip around the edge of crust. Press down and crimp to seal.

USE LITTLE LIQUID Good pastry uses as little liquid as possible to get the dough in shape. Use very cold milk or water and knead the dough lightly. For a flaky crust, place in a well-heated oven as soon as ready.

TO GLAZE CRUST Fifteen minutes before pie is to be removed from the oven, brush with either the beaten yolk of one egg; an unbeaten egg white, or with milk.

Or, for an attractive, sugary topping, sprinkle the top crust with a light coating of sugar or a sugar-cinnamon mixture.

61

USE A MARBLE SLAB   If your kitchen boasts a marble slab for candy-making, use it to roll out pie crust in order to keep the dough as cool as possible.

HANDLE LIGHTLY   Handle pie crust as lightly as possible, kneading only enough to make dough hold together and touching as little as possible. Roll with a quick, light motion, rolling away from you.

FOR FLAKIER PASTRY   For a flakier pastry, add the shortening in two parts. Add the first half of the fat to the flour, cutting it in until the mixture looks like coarse cornmeal. Then cut in the remaining half of the fat until the flour-fat particles are the size of small peas. Then add the liquid, a little at a time until the dough holds together. Press the dampened dough into a ball and chill. Bake in a preheated oven.

TO ROLL OUT   Chill pastry dough 15 to 20 minutes before rolling, for easier handling. Use a light hand on the rolling pin. Roll on a lightly-floured board and turn several times to prevent sticking. Cut the rolled pastry one inch larger than the pie pan and fold back the excess dough around rim to seal edges of two-crust pie or to make a fluted edge of a one-crust pie.